eland

Glasgow
Liverpool
London

ESTERN
ROACHES

EUROPE

Gibraltar

AFRICA

Freetown

Year	Number of ships sunk	Tonnage sunk	Number of U-boats sunk
1940	349	1,805,494	23
1941	496	2,421,700	35
1942	1,006	5,471,222	86
1943	285	1,659,601	237
1944	31	175,013	242
1945	19	122,729	151

Cape Town

Series 117

This is a Ladybird Expert book, one of a series of titles for an adult readership. Written by some of the leading lights and outstanding communicators in their fields and published by one of the most trusted and well-loved names in books, the Ladybird Expert series provides clear, accessible and authoritative introductions, informed by expert opinion, to key subjects drawn from science, history and culture.

The Publisher would like to thank the following for the illustrative references for this book:
Page 15: © IWM (A 4545); page 33: the Crypto Museum; page 45: © Corbis/Getty Images

Every effort has been made to ensure images are correctly attributed; however, if any omission or error has been made please notify the Publisher for correction in future editions.

MICHAEL JOSEPH

UK | USA | Canada | Ireland | Australia
India | New Zealand | South Africa

Michael Joseph is part of the Penguin Random House group of companies
whose addresses can be found at global.penguinrandomhouse.com

Penguin
Random House
UK

First published 2018
001

Text copyright © James Holland, 2018

All images copyright © Ladybird Books Ltd, 2018

The moral right of the author has been asserted

Printed in Italy by L.E.G.O. S.p.A.

A CIP catalogue record for this book is available from the British Library
ISBN: 978-0-718-18631-9

www.greenpenguin.co.uk

The Battle of the Atlantic

James Holland

**with illustrations by
Keith Burns**

Ladybird Books Ltd, London

The Atlantic battle began just a few hours after war was declared by Britain and France on 3 September 1939. Some 370 miles north-west of Ireland, a German submarine, or U-boat, *U-30*, spotted a large vessel steaming west. Lieutenant Fritz Lemp, *U-30*'s commander, was convinced it was an armed merchant cruiser and so opened fire with two torpedoes. These struck at 7.40 p.m., and just after midnight the ship finally sank along with 128 men, women and children. Tragically, the boat was not armed at all, but had been a small transatlantic liner, the SS *Athenia*, heading to America from Britain with civilians fleeing the war.

It was the start of the longest battle of the entire Second World War, in which ships, submarines and aircraft fought a bitter war of attrition that saw the deaths of over 100,000 servicemen and civilians. Those fighting across these brutal grey seas also fought an ongoing battle with the ocean itself. The Atlantic is a vast and unforgiving place. This was also, in the context of six years of war, possibly the most important battle of them all, because without supplies, warring nations cannot fight. For the Axis forces to defeat the Allies, those supply lines across the ocean had to be severed.

Sinking the *Athenia* was against 'Prize' rules, which forbade the sinking of civilian passenger vessels during armed conflict and to which Germany had agreed. For Britain, that the ship was sunk by a U-boat also had worrying echoes of the First World War, when German submarines had severely affected the flow of transatlantic supplies. Britain was utterly dependent on seaborne trade, so severing those sea lanes was an overwhelming priority for Germany's war.

At the same time, the Germans also knew that, the moment war was declared, Britain's vastly superior navy would impose an economic blockade against Germany – which was precisely what they did. This was comparatively easy for the Royal Navy to do because Germany was stuck in central Europe with only a comparatively short coastline, so access to the world's oceans was very limited.

The most obvious way to break through such a blockade was by submarine. Technology in U-boats had advanced significantly since the last war, and with Germany's poor natural resources and geographical isolation, combined with demands for a large army and air force, it made sense for its navy, the Kriegsmarine, to focus almost entirely on developing as sizeable a U-boat fleet as possible. U-boats were also smaller, easier and cheaper in every regard to build and keep in fuel than a large surface fleet.

Despite this obvious logic, however, Hitler, the German Führer, had backed the so-called 'Z Plan' to build a fleet of battleships, aircraft carriers, cruisers and destroyers. Only a fraction of these had been constructed by September 1939.

HMS *Hood* leads HMS *Rodney* and HMS *Renown* on manoeuvres on the High Seas.

The British responded to the sinking of *Athenia* by immediately imposing the convoy system, whereby a mass of merchant ships sailed together protected by escorting warships. These were mostly destroyers: fast, manoeuvrable vessels that were much smaller than the larger cruisers and battleships known as 'capital ships'. Destroyers were equipped with depth-charges – mines that sank beneath the surface and then exploded – as well as with guns and torpedoes. The theory was that these escorts would provide a protective screen, while the merchant ships would also benefit from safety in numbers. It was very hard to protect a lone vessel sailing across the Atlantic.

Convoys did cause problems, however, because they meant a mass of ships departed and arrived at port at the same time, and needed loading and unloading all at once too. In between, dockworkers had little to do. It was not an efficient use of port facilities, but unquestionably made the ships' passage safer.

As German troops swarmed over Poland, the Kriegsmarine's new surface fleet was largely stuck behind the British blockade. Not so the U-boats, however. In September, one of the Royal Navy's precious aircraft carriers, HMS *Courageous*, was sunk. Then, in October, in one of the most daring and skilled attacks of the war, Lieutenant Günther Prien of *U-47* managed to slip into the narrow and heavily protected British base at Scapa Flow in the Orkneys and sink the mighty battleship *Royal Oak*, with the loss of 833 men. It was a severe shock not just to the navy but to Britain as a whole.

These attacks showed all too clearly what a potent force U-boats could be, yet at the war's start Admiral Karl Dönitz, the commander of the BdU, the U-boat arm, had just 57 rather than the 300 for which he had been pleading. Even this small number looked more impressive on paper than it was in reality, because submarines operated to the rule of thirds: one third at sea, one third heading to and from their hunting grounds, and one third undergoing re-equipping and repairs. In all, there were only 3,000 men in the entire BdU and few more than fifty U-boat commanders. Training took time, as did building up the necessary skill and experience. Should Dönitz ever have the chance to increase the size of his force significantly, the pool of manpower for such an expansion was very slight indeed.

The trouble was, Hitler was a continentalist and understood naval power even less than he did land warfare. Building a surface fleet was more about his monstrous ego than anything. Certainly, the mighty battleship *Bismarck* looked a lot more impressive than a Mk VII U-boat, the mainstay of the BdU. Just a handful of U-boats were operating in the Atlantic in the opening months of the war and yet these few were demonstrating all too clearly the potential they possessed. A hundred U-boats operating together, rather than fewer than ten, would certainly have greatly hindered Britain and France's ongoing war effort.

Hitler launches the mighty battleship *Bismarck*.

Germany was keenly aware that it was short of resources, which was why the Prussian and then, after 1871, the German approach to war was always to try to win as quickly as possible and to avoid a long, drawn-out conflict at all costs. The four-year attrition of the First World War had shown only too clearly these fundamental shortcomings. Back then, the Royal Navy's blockade had crippled the country, and it now threatened to do so again.

Britain, by contrast, not only had the largest empire the world had ever known, but also possessions beyond her empire. Much of Argentina, for example, from cattle farms and meat factories to the railway system, was owned by British companies. Britain also had the world's largest navy and merchant navy, and access to more than 80 per cent of the world's merchant shipping. These tens of thousands of ships were delivering supplies from all around the globe.

Furthermore, the world's largest oil producers, and by some margin, were the USA and Venezuela, both in the west. And whether timber and rubber from the Far East, copper and bauxite from Africa, or oil and food from the Americas, all this shipping reached Britain via the Atlantic.

Britain's navy was the country's Senior Service and its pre-war size ensured there was now a greater pool of experience and skill to spread during rapid wartime expansion. There were also the shipyards and shipbuilding skills to continue the flow of new vessels, while on the other side of the Atlantic lay Canada, a British dominion. The Canadians were to play a crucial part in this battle.

Battle of the Atlantic, Mar-Dec 1941
- Allied shipping sunk
- U-boats sunk

Despite the loss of *Royal Oak* and *Courageous*, the British were not especially worried by the U-boat threat in the early months of the war. Britain alone had over 10,000 merchant vessels, while there were barely ten U-boats ever operating at one time in the entire expanse of the Atlantic.

The British also had good intelligence and infrastructure, which included a global organization called the Naval Control of Shipping, which tracked the movements, cargoes and destinations of almost all Allied shipping. Naval intelligence was overseen by the Operational Intelligence Centre, which in turn drew on a number of sources of intelligence, including the Government Code and Cypher School at Bletchley Park, where civilian mathematicians and scientists were working on cracking enemy signal codes. It was also served by a network of Radio Intercept Stations and reports from around the world sent via secure underwater telegraph cables known as the VESCA system.

A further source of intelligence came from the crews of the Royal Air Force's Coastal Command. U-boats were not proper submarines, but rather 'submersibles', and could only fully submerge for a short period of time and at much reduced speed. This meant they mostly travelled on the surface and so, as convoys entered the Western Approaches – the part of the Atlantic off the west coast of the British Isles – aircraft could scan the waters around them and, if they spotted a U-boat, drive it under the surface where it would immediately lose speed.

These systems collectively ensured that it was, in theory at any rate, possible to know exactly where any ship was at any moment of any given day. The challenge now was to work out where the U-boats were as well.

The Operations Room at the HQ of the Royal Navy's Western Approaches Command.

While the tiny U-boat force attempted to form itself into 'Wolfpacks' of six at a time operating together off the west coast of Ireland, the German surface fleet remained in port, hardly daring to venture out. In October, the battle-cruiser *Gneisenau* headed into the North Sea, but as soon as she learned the British Home Fleet had picked up her movement, she hurried back again.

Meanwhile, three U-boats were sunk in October alone and nine by the end of the year – a significant number considering the size of the BdU. In December, the small 'pocket' battleship *Graf Spee* managed to break through the British blockade and sink three Allied freighters, but was then chased all the way south across the Atlantic to the River Plate in Argentina. Cornered, the *Graf Spee* was then scuttled to avoid being captured. Her demise rather underlined the folly of taking on a much larger and more proficient navy with lesser capital ships.

On the other hand, the small U-boat force continued to sink significant numbers of Allied merchant ships – albeit mostly independents operating outside the convoys. Fifty-six ships were sunk in February 1940, for example. Little was happening in the war on the land, but there could be no doubting that the war at sea was now well under way.

The *Graf Spee* under attack from the Royal Navy.

In April, the war at sea shifted to the waters around Norway, where the Germans had invaded, and then, at the end of May, came the evacuation of British and Allied troops from Dunkirk and elsewhere in France. With the fall of France in the third week of June and the end of the Norwegian campaign, the U-boats were sent back to the Atlantic, while fast German torpedo boats – *Schnellboote* – together with the Luftwaffe, the German air force, turned their attention to British coastal shipping. Many supplies, particularly coal, travelled in small convoys down the east and along the south coasts. They were now pummelled by the Germans.

At the same time, Britain was preparing for a possible German invasion and so Admiral Sir Dudley Pound, the First Sea Lord – the head of the Royal Navy – insisted the Home Fleet should concentrate in the south and south-east in case the Germans attempted a seaborne crossing of the Channel. Admiral Sir Charles Forbes, commander-in-chief of the Home Fleet, believed this concentration of force was overly cautious. He rightly argued that, so long as the RAF was still flying, the Germans would never be able to launch an invasion in secret and that there would always be time to send warships from the Western Approaches to the Channel. He also pointed out there were now large numbers of trawlers and lighters, newly armed, which were part of the Royal Navy Patrol Service. Better known as 'Harry Tate's Navy', these tough trawlermen were sweeping German mines in the Channel, laying their own and keeping watch for an invasion.

German torpedo boats – *Schnellboote* – speed across the Channel.

Forbes' arguments fell on deaf ears, much to Britain's cost. The convoys crossing the Atlantic were now doing so with almost no escorts. Most were entering port on the west coast, at Liverpool or Greenock in Scotland, and so, despite the vast size of the ocean, U-boats could safely lie in wait in the Western Approaches and know they were likely to intercept them. Convoys at this stage of the war never exceeded thirty-five ships but were spaced in columns around 600 metres apart, with each vessel roughly 400 metres behind the other, so they covered a sizeable area. The smoke from their stacks could be seen for miles around. Intercepting them was still no simple matter, but certainly the U-boats had never had easier prey than these unprotected convoys.

Throughout 1940, there were never more than fourteen U-boats operating in the Atlantic at one time, but in June they sank 134 boats, in July 102 and in August 91, amounting to more than a million tons of shipping. One of those relishing the slaughter was Lieutenant Teddy Suhren, the torpedo officer on *U-48*. By 20 June, they had been on patrol for more than three weeks and had already sunk seven ships. Suhren then spotted a tanker and, a little after 5.30 p.m., having made the calculations of distance, course and speed, he fired a torpedo from 5,000 metres. This was a massive distance. 'No one believed it would hit,' recorded Suhren. But it did, and the Dutch tanker *Moordrecht* exploded in a massive fireball and sank.

While the Battle of Britain raged over southern England, out in the Atlantic the high number of sinkings continued. This period became known as the 'Happy Time' by the U-boat crews, yet despite this, not once did Admiral Dönitz's U-boat fleet sink anything like the half million tons in one month he reckoned was needed to bring Britain to its knees – the most had been 375,000 tons in June. As it was, the magic 500,000-ton monthly total was based on the assumption that Britain would have to continue to import more than 80 per cent of its food, as had been the case before the war.

Already, though, Britain had begun to turn that around with a major revolution in agriculture. Much open grassland had been ploughed up for crops and the number of livestock reduced. Limited rationing – far less severe than in Germany, for example – was introduced, which ensured everyone was provided with a balanced diet. At the same time, the increased food production on British farms meant more shipping space was freed up for the resources needed to build weapons. Bad though the losses in the Atlantic were, they were nothing like enough to prevent Britain carrying on the fight, let alone force her to end the war.

At the same time, German imports were down as much as 80 per cent on pre-war figures as a direct consequence of the British blockade. That was a problem because it meant Germany had to look elsewhere for those all-important resources.

A Land Girl ploughs a field.

None the less, just a handful of U-boats had sunk a huge amount of Allied shipping, including, on 14 December, the unescorted *Western Prince*, carrying cargo and passengers. One of those rescued was Cyril Thompson, a ship designer from Sunderland who had been in the USA to try to get the Americans to start building a new type of easy-to-construct merchant ship he had designed. A deal had been struck with the US government and an entrepreneur called Henry Kaiser, who promised to construct two new shipyards specially for the task. Thompson made it back safely and continued to build his first such boat in Sunderland. It would be called *Empire Liberty*, and from this all such vessels became known as 'Liberty ships'. Henry Kaiser pledged to produce each in just over 200 days. British and American shipbuilders were now joining forces.

Time was working against Germany. The 'Happy Time' had shown all too clearly what might have been achieved had Admiral Dönitz had the kind of numbers of U-boats he'd demanded. Instead, the mighty battleships lay idle in port, doing very little, although a lone pocket battleship, *Admiral Scheer*, did manage to slip unseen into the Atlantic, sink five ships and hurry back again.

With the failure to bring Britain to heel, Hitler had begun preparing for the invasion of the Soviet Union far earlier than he had originally intended. This was now Germany's main focus rather than the Atlantic, where, in January 1941, just six U-boats were operating. What's more, Allied convoys already had much increased numbers of escorts, and from shipyards in America, Britain and Canada more were arriving too.

Cyril Thompson shows the Americans blueprints for his 'Liberty' ship design.

On 3 February 1941, the German cruisers *Gneisenau* and *Scharnhorst* managed to slip through the Royal Navy's blockade and head out into the Atlantic, where they continued to evade the British Home Fleet. It was a dent to British pride and Prime Minister Winston Churchill, for one, was set on revenge. The Battle of the Atlantic, he declared, was to receive top priority.

And so it was. Before the war, Britain had very sensibly focused on building and upgrading larger ships, but now most warship construction was of destroyers and even smaller corvettes. By the start of 1941, the Royal Navy could call on 126 destroyers, 39 sloops and 89 corvettes for Western Approaches Command alone. RAF Coastal Command was now using longer-range aircraft, and both aircraft and ships were starting to be equipped with small onboard radar sets. This was possible because of the British invention of the cavity magnetron, a device that dramatically reduced the size needed for effective radar detection. The cavity magnetron was not known about by the Germans.

Western Approaches HQ in Liverpool was also re-equipped and developed, and by February 1941 was a much-improved new operations centre, while escort groups of destroyers and corvettes were introduced to protect the precious convoys. 'The U-boat at sea must be hunted,' Churchill had declared, and 'the U-boat in the building-yard or dock must be bombed.'

The results were not long in coming.

An RAF Sunderland – known as the 'Flying Porcupine' – circles a U-boat.

In March, *U-47*, commanded by Günther Prien, was sunk with the loss of all hands, as was Joachim Schepke's *U-100*, while Otto Kreschmer's *U-99* was also sunk and the crew captured. These were three of the U-boat arm's most skilled, successful and celebrated aces and, because of the BdU's small size, were blows from which it would not easily recover. In all, five U-boats were sunk in March 1941.

Further setbacks followed for the Germans. That same month, German naval cypher materials were captured by British commandos during an attack on the Norwegian Lofoten Islands. Then, in May, *U-110* was captured in the Atlantic along with its Enigma coding machine and, crucially, its code books. The Germans did not know about the capture of either. British cryptanalysts at Bletchley Park could use these prizes to start deciphering German naval signal traffic. The benefits of this breakthrough were potentially enormous.

Also in May 1941, the mighty battleship *Bismarck* and heavy cruiser *Prinz Eugen* escaped the blockade and headed into the Atlantic. The Home Fleet hurried after them and in the first exchange of fire *Bismarck* sank the battlecruiser HMS *Hood*. It was a short-lived victory, however, as Royal Navy aircraft torpedoed the battleship, jamming her rudder and leaving her circling helplessly. British battleships and cruisers closed in for the kill and soon after *Bismarck* was sent to the bottom. *Prinz Eugen* managed to escape back to Brest, but not one German capital ship ever dipped into the grey, bitter seas of the Atlantic again.

A torpedo-carrying Royal Navy Fairey Swordfish attacks the *Bismarck*.

In the opening eighteen months of the war, a lack of mid-Atlantic refuelling bases, combined with a shortage of escorts, had meant there was a large section in the middle of the ocean where the convoys were on their own and vulnerable. In April 1941, however, Allied naval and air bases finally opened in Iceland, which meant the British could now escort convoys as far as 35° west – a huge improvement. Then, in May, the rapidly growing Royal Canadian Navy agreed to close the final gap all the way to Newfoundland. It was another crucial marker in Canada's huge commitment to the war, and one that was out of all proportion to the small size of its population of just over 10 million.

There were now some eighty Canadian corvettes in service, or nearly so. The crews lacked the training and experience of the Royal Navy, but this was hardly surprising considering their navy had grown from just 3,000 personnel at the war's start. In the vicious seas of the north-west Atlantic they would soon learn, however. At any rate, from now on the Canadians, volunteers all, would escort transatlantic convoys to what was called the Mid-Ocean Meeting Point, then head to Iceland for refuelling before escorting another convoy back.

There were also now over 200 aircraft operating from Iceland. For the aircrews, anti-U-boat patrols were thankless: long hours scanning a vast and often empty sea. But they were making a difference, pushing Dönitz's U-boats further west to the one part of the ocean aircraft still could not reach: the mid-Atlantic.

Corvettes in the mid-Atlantic.

In August 1941, Winston Churchill and the US President, Franklin D. Roosevelt, along with their respective chiefs of staff – senior military commanders – met at Placentia Bay off the Canadian coast for what became known as the Atlantic Conference. By this time, American factories were just starting to produce significant amounts of war materiel, much of which was heading to Britain, while Henry Kaiser's new shipyards were already constructing the new Liberty ships. America was still not in the war, but during these meetings Roosevelt did agree that the US Navy should now join the Battle of the Atlantic and play a part in protecting Allied shipping.

A month later, the US Navy's Atlantic Fleet, although still officially neutral, was out at sea, escorting convoys as far as the Mid-Ocean Meeting Point with the Canadians now under their command. Among those Americans serving in the Atlantic was Hollywood star Douglas Fairbanks Jr. 'What the hell had I got myself into?' he wondered as he first headed out on to the ocean.

Meanwhile, cryptanalysts at Bletchley Park were now able to decode Enigma signals traffic with greater speed, enabling convoys to avoid the U-boats and giving the RAF a narrower area to search. This intelligence, combined with improved escorts, meant shipping losses had fallen dramatically. Dönitz now sent his U-boats deeper into the mid-Atlantic and on 9 September they found and struck Convoy SC42. Although protected by the Canadians, the escorts lacked both modern anti-submarine warfare equipment (ASW) and experience. Fifteen freighters were lost in two days.

The Bombe codebreaking computer at Bletchley Park.

Bad though those losses were, Dönitz's U-boats were by this time sinking just 66 tons of shipping per U-boat per day, a figure that had been 727 tons a year earlier. At the same time, Dönitz now reckoned his U-boats needed to sink a massive 800,000 tons of Allied shipping per month, up 300,000 tons from his estimation at the start of the war. So far, they had yet to achieve half that. Well over 80 per cent of all convoys were getting through unscathed. Escort group commanders like Lieutenant-Commander Donald Macintyre, who had captured U-boat ace Otto Kretschmer back in May 1941, had a mass of experience and were sailing aboard destroyers equipped with the latest radar; Macintyre barely had a single loss on his watch. With every passing month, more Allied ships were being upgraded.

On 31 October 1941, the Germans suffered another setback when *U-552* sank an American destroyer, *Reuben James*, not realizing it was a neutral vessel. The American public were shocked and outraged by the news; the United States' entry into the war had been brought a step closer. For the U-boat's commander, Erich Topp, it was a long journey back to base after he realized what he had done. 'The tension a man endures when he thinks he is making history,' he noted, 'however unintentional, is indeed enormous.'

As it turned out, Topp need not have worried unduly, because just over a month later the Japanese attacked the US Pacific Fleet at Pearl Harbor in Hawaii, and the United States was suddenly in the war for good.

Captain Erich Topp on the bridge of *U-552* about to fire on the *Reuben James*.

At the start of 1942, Dönitz had 91 operational U-boats, although 23 were in the Mediterranean on Hitler's direct orders – and against Dönitz's wishes – and 60 per cent were undergoing repairs, which left only a dozen for patrols in the Atlantic. The British had also introduced escort carriers – ships hastily converted to carry a flight deck. Among those flying US-built Martlets on the escort carrier *Audacity* was Lieutenant Eric 'Winkle' Brown. The flight deck was just 100 metres long, but Brown quickly mastered the technique of taking off and landing back again. During escort duty to and from Gibraltar, he managed to shoot down two of the Luftwaffe's precious Focke-Wulf Condors, four-engine transports converted to become maritime bombers and operating from airfields along the Biscay coast. Brown's technique was to fly directly towards the Condor, firing at the cockpit.

Audacity's luck soon ran out, however, when on 21 December she was hit by three torpedoes fired from *U-751*. 'Literally,' said Brown, 'the bows fell off the ship.' He himself was very lucky to survive and was eventually picked up from the water.

Two and a half years into the battle, another shift was now about to take place. The British were no longer cracking Enigma codes as quickly, while American entry into the war had actually made the Allied position in the Atlantic weaker, because the US Navy immediately sent most of its warships to the Pacific to combat the Japanese threat. What's more, the shipping lanes off the coast of America, into the Gulf of Mexico and down through the Caribbean to Brazil and Argentina were some of the most congested in the world. Here, American coastal shipping was sailing independently, unescorted and through a series of narrow straits between strings of islands. For the U-boats these represented rich pickings. Another slaughter swiftly began to unfold.

Crossing the width of the Atlantic meant much longer patrols for the U-boat crews. Now patrolling off the American coast was Teddy Suhren, commanding his own boat, *U-564*. He and his crew sank two of seventy-one ships sent to the bottom in February. In March, ninety-two were sunk. The answer was to increase air patrols and establish a convoy system, but this could not be done overnight, and so the carnage off America continued.

Life at sea was tough enough to break any man, physically and mentally. The crew of a U-boat lived in cramped, primitive conditions. Water had to be very carefully rationed, so no one could wash or shave. A U-boat soon stank of sweat, oil, mildew and rotten food. Long periods of boredom were followed by moments of high tension and fear. Being stalked by a destroyer was terrifying: under the surface it was impossible to see their enemy, but around them depth-charges would explode, causing the U-boat to shake and roll. Any moment might be their last.

Merchant crews were extremely vulnerable and had to depend on others for their safety. Just like the crew of a hunted U-boat, merchant sailors never knew when they might be struck by an enemy torpedo. Luck played a huge part. Those lost at sea were rarely recovered, and most faced a lonely death.

Conditions were often brutal. Even in summer, crews could find themselves in the middle of a storm with waves crashing over them. In winter, it was also frequently freezing cold, especially in the northern Atlantic. Out on deck or on the ship's bridge, they were exposed to wind, rain, sea spray and thunderous waves. Once soaked, it was hard to get dry again. Donald Macintyre reckoned that on one winter escort patrol he had not been dry once. Not for nothing was the Atlantic known as the cruel sea.

The first US coastal convoy sailed in May 1942, but it was still a while longer before the whole East Coast shipping system was put into convoy and, with increased numbers of U-boats finally reaching Dönitz's force, the slaughter continued, with 125 ships sunk in May and a staggering 144 in June, of which 121 had still been sailing independently.

Even so, this second 'Happy Time' for the U-boats was largely a false resurgence: it was a self-inflicted wound by the Americans rather than a leap forward in technology. A potentially game-changing new U-boat had been successfully tested back in 1940 – one that was a proper submarine rather than a submersible, and which could travel at 23 knots under water, faster than any freighter. But investment lagged and it was still not in production. Otherwise, the most common U-boat, the Type VII, had barely moved forward at all. Nor had torpedoes much improved. There had been some signals developments, but not at a pace that was outstripping the Allies.

Meanwhile, Allied technology most definitely was improving. There were now many more 'Very Long Range' aircraft flying over the Atlantic, equipped not only with radar but also with powerful spotlights so they could operate at night. In July, Teddy Suhren and his crew on *U-564* were on patrol once more and were repeatedly spotted and forced to dive. 'Up and down the whole time,' he wrote. 'It's like being in a lift! These fiendish air patrols of the Allies!'

A B-24 Liberator attacks a U-boat.

In Britain the harvest of 1942 was a bumper one. British farmers had produced 46 million tons of grain in 1939, but that had now almost doubled. In contrast, in Germany each harvest had been down on those before the war. Dönitz's U-boats had sunk 636,926 tons of Allied shipping in June, mostly off America, but total imports to Britain had barely dipped: 2,006,000 tons had arrived in January, and an increased 2,214,000 in May, despite the carnage off America.

In July, with increased air cover and convoys, plus the drain of such huge distances to contend with, Dönitz sent his U-boats back to the mid-Atlantic, where their pickings dropped dramatically. Donald Macintyre was commanding a new ship equipped with the latest radar and also 'Huff-Duff' – high-frequency direction finding – which picked up radio signals from U-boats. These interceptions enabled the destroyers to work out the location from where the signals were being sent. Armed with this, an escort or aircraft could then go hunting for the U-boat. It was almost certainly down to Huff-Duff that Teddy Suhren's July patrol was so frequently interrupted.

What's more, this improved technology was being harnessed to increased experience and, with it, skill, amongst both British and Canadian crews. U-boats had concentrated on sinking merchant ships rather than escorts, so the number of Allied naval losses in the Atlantic was slight. Dönitz, meanwhile, at long last had over 200 operational U-boats, and even more on their way, but most of his experienced crews had gone.

The hunters were increasingly becoming the hunted.

A Royal Navy 'Huff-Duff' operator.

In January 1943, Churchill, Roosevelt and the British and American chiefs of staff met at the Casablanca Conference in Morocco, where they agreed that defeating the U-boat menace was their top priority. Both Britain and America wanted to win the war as quickly as possible and at the least cost, and by using machinery and technology so that the number of men risking their lives at the front line could be kept to a minimum. At the time of the conference, Anglo-US forces were battling in North Africa, but they intended to invade Sicily in the summer and France the following year, in 1944. The foundation of that strategy and of all long-term planning, however, was shipping, because everything, from fuel to tanks, food, ammunition and medical supplies, was brought overseas by ship. But with ever more U-boats now massing in the Atlantic, that smooth flow of supplies was under threat. The Allied war chiefs agreed it was one that had to be destroyed.

Fortunately, the Allies had once again cracked the German naval Enigma codes. What's more, they were continuing to win the technological battle. New weapons were rapidly being thrown into the fight, from acoustic homing torpedoes to rockets with armour-piercing warheads, and superb new American 10cm wavelength radar. Donald Macintyre's ship and other escorts were being equipped with 'Hedgehog'. This new piece of weaponry threw out a pattern of twenty-four contact-fused bombs ahead of a ship hunting a U-boat. It was more accurate than firing off depth-charges.

At the same time, Dönitz was still waiting for his new generation U-boat. He was rapidly running out of time.

Roosevelt and Churchill in Casablanca.

Meanwhile, shipyards in Britain and America were continuing to build ever more Liberty ships, and in the United States these were now being launched at an astonishing rate. The first had been constructed in over 200 days, but by July 1942 one had been built in just 43 days and by August another in just 24 days. Then, in September, the *Joseph N. Teal* had been finished in a staggering 10 days. Two months later, the *Robert E. Peary* was completed in just 4 days, 15 hours and 26 minutes.

How could the U-boats, with their still-failing torpedoes and lack of sufficient air cover, possibly compete? The answer, of course, was that they could not.

More ships than ever were now sailing across the Atlantic in larger convoys with greater numbers of escorts with improved weaponry, and with more air protection. New support groups were also being thrown into the battle: fast, well-equipped destroyers whose job was not to protect convoys but to hunt U-boats.

The only downturn the Allies had to overcome was the change in Enigma codes, which meant they were taking too long to crack to have any effect. By March, there were some seventy U-boats in the Atlantic, and with their own improved signals intelligence they were getting the highest interception rates of the war. Two convoys, HX229 and SC122, were particularly hard hit when forty U-boats attacked them. The mid-Atlantic was awash with flotsam and debris as one merchant ship after another went down.

A Liberty ship under construction.

March 1943 may have looked like a bad month for the Allies as 633,731 tons of shipping was lost, but the U-boats were now largely corralled into the mid-Atlantic while increased air operations over the Bay of Biscay harried their movement to and from their bases. In May, forty-one U-boats were destroyed, and among the young German submariners gone for ever was Dönitz's only son. Meanwhile, of the 370 merchantmen that sailed, only six were sunk. The U-boat threat had been neutralized. 'Wolfpack operations against convoys in the North Atlantic, the main theatre of operations,' recorded Dönitz, 'were no longer possible.' On 24 May, he ordered them all to withdraw, and with the utmost caution. 'We had lost the Battle of the Atlantic.'

Dönitz was right: the battle had been lost, but that was not the end of the U-boats. Not yet. Over the summer of 1943, he deployed most of them west and south of the Azores, hoping they would snare Allied convoys heading to the Mediterranean. He also sent some to the south Atlantic. New weapons and shipping detectors had been promised. Perhaps they would help him yet turn the tables.

At the same time, the Allies were coordinating efforts even more fully and effectively. The Canadians had massively grown in strength and experience, while the US re-entered the Atlantic battle with the formation of the Tenth Fleet at the end of April. Intelligence efforts were also coordinated and properly shared. Good intelligence, combined with massively superior forces and weaponry, ensured the U-boats would soon be crushed once and for all.

The oily remains of another U-boat sent to the bottom.

This superiority was demonstrated on 8 July 1943 when a newly equipped Very Long Range RAF Liberator spotted *U-514* off the Spanish coast and so turned in to attack, first with eight armour-piercing rockets, then with eight depth-charges which exploded all around the stricken U-boat. Finally, as *U-514* began to sink, the crew released their homing torpedo. A huge underwater explosion erupted and the U-boat disappeared for ever.

This was the kind of sophisticated weaponry the inexperienced U-boat crews now had to contend with. Only latterly had Hitler accepted the need for a much larger fleet of U-boats. New weapons were also arriving in the summer of 1943, but by then it was too little too late. The novice crews were getting slaughtered. By the autumn, Allied victory over the U-boats was complete.

U-boats continued to patrol until the end of the war, and still achieved some successes, but the losses continued to mount. In the final weeks, Dönitz even managed to launch the new generation Type XXI U-boats. By then, almost three-quarters of all U-boat men had been killed.

In truth, the U-boats had never come close to winning. Just 1.4 per cent of all Allied sailings across the Atlantic had been sunk. Even during the 'Happy Times', the U-boats had fallen well short of their monthly targets, which in turn had never been enough. Greater industrial output and far greater prioritization by the Allies had ensured that in this most crucial of theatres, they had won a crushing victory.

From the outset, the Allies had understood the vital importance of the Atlantic. The same could not be said for Nazi Germany. It cost them the war.

The attack on the *U-514*.

Further Reading

GENERAL HISTORIES

James Holland *The War in the West: The Rise of Germany, 1939–1941* (Corgi, 2016)

James Holland *The War in the West: The Allies Fight Back, 1941–1943* (Bantam Press, 2017)

Marc Milner *The Battle of the Atlantic* (History Press, 2016)

Donald Macintyre *The Battle of the Atlantic* (Pen & Sword Maritime, 2014)

MEMOIRS

Donald Macintyre *U-Boat Killer* (Cassell, 1999)

Teddy Suhren *Teddy Suhren: Ace of Aces* (Frontline Books, 2011)

NOVELS

Nicholas Montserrat *The Cruel Sea* (Penguin Books, 2009)

Lothar Günther Buchheim *Das Boot* (Orion, 2013)